Languages of the World

Polish

Lucia Raatma

Heinemann Library
Chicago, Illinois

www.heinemannraintree.com
Visit our website to find out more information about Heinemann-Raintree books.

To order:
☎ Phone 888-454-2279
▭ Visit www.heinemannraintree.com to browse our catalog and order online.

©2012 Heinemann Library
an imprint of Capstone Global Library, LLC
Chicago, Illinois

Edited by Dan Nunn, Rebecca Rissman, and Catherine Veitch
Designed by Marcus Bell
Picture research by Ruth Blair
Production by Victoria Fitzgerald
Originated by Capstone Global Library Ltd
Printed and bound in China by South China Printing Company Ltd

15 14 13 12 11
10 9 8 7 6 5 4 3 2 1

Library of Congress Cataloging-in-Publication Data
Raatma, Lucia.
   Polish / Lucia Tarbox Raatma.
      p. cm.—(Languages of the world)
   Includes bibliographical references and index.
   ISBN 978-1-4329-5083-5—ISBN 978-1-4329-5090-3 (pbk.) 1. Polish language—Textbooks for foreign speakers—English. 2. Polish language—Grammar. 3. Polish language—Spoken Polish. I. Title.
   PG6129.E5R33 2012
   491'.8582421—dc22   2010043789

Acknowledgments
We would like to thank the following for permission to reproduce photographs: Alamy pp. 5 (© Julio Etchart), 7 (© Brigette Sullivan/Outer Focus Photos); Corbis pp. 11 (© Radoslaw Pietruszka/PAP), 22 (© Miroslaw Trembecki/PAP), 24 (© Juan Francisco Moreno/epa), 29 (© Ian Trower/JAI); iStockphoto p. 15 (© Igor Stepovik); Photolibrary pp. 23 (Peter Arkell), 28 (Superstock); Shutterstock pp. 6 (© Monkey Business Images), 8 (© Miau), 9 (© c.), 10 (© blueking), 12 (© Golden Pixels LLC), 13 (© ImageryMajestic), 14 (© jadimages), 16 (© Dmitriy Shironosov), 17 (© Zurijeta), 18 (© katatonia82), 19 (© mkasperski), 20 (© privilege), 21 (© stefanolunardi), 25 (© Stanislaw Tokarski), 26 (© barbaradudzinska), 27 (© Taratorki).

Cover photograph of a young girl reproduced with permission of iStockphoto (© Krystian Kaczmarski).

We would like to thank Dorota Holowiak for her invaluable help in the preparation of this book.

Every effort has been made to contact copyright holders of material reproduced in this book. Any omissions will be rectified in subsequent printings if notice is given to the publisher.

All the Internet addresses (URLs) given in this book were valid at the time of going to press. However, due to the dynamic nature of the Internet, some addresses may have changed, or sites may have changed or ceased to exist since publication. While the author and publisher regret any inconvenience this may cause readers, no responsibility for any such changes can be accepted by either the author or the publisher.

Contents

Polish words are in italics, *like this*. You can find out how to say them by looking in the pronunciation guide.

Polish Around the World

The Polish language is spoken all over the world. It is the main language of Poland. Some people also speak Polish in other countries in Europe, such as Slovakia, Ukraine, Russia, and Romania.

Poland

Poland is in Europe.

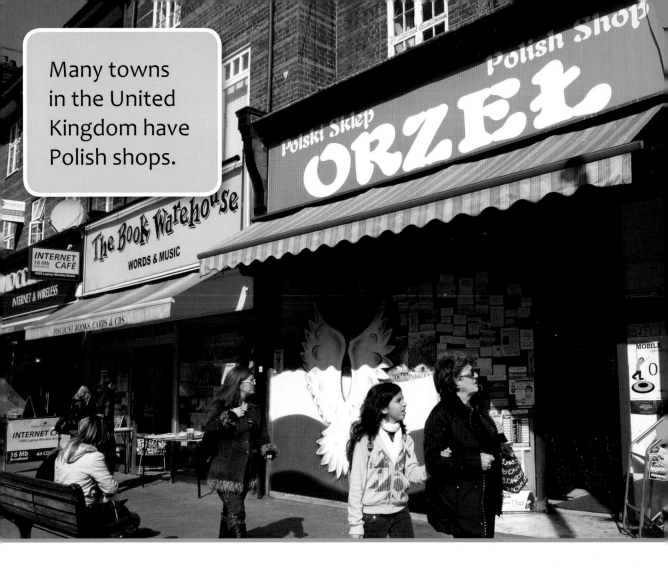

Many towns in the United Kingdom have Polish shops.

There are many Polish speakers in the United Kingdom and the United States, too. Some people speak Polish in Australia and Brazil as well.

Who Speaks Polish?

There are about 40 million Polish speakers in the world. In Poland, nearly everyone speaks Polish. But there are different types, or dialects, of Polish in different parts of the country.

These people are taking part in a Polish festival in Chicago, Illinois.

In the United States there are about nine million people who have a Polish background. Some of them still speak Polish.

Polish and English

You may already know some Polish words. Many English words are so well known that they are part of the Polish language now. Some examples are *parking*, *jazz*, and *weekend*.

The word *jazz*, a type of music, is now part of the Polish language.

The English word "parking" has become part of the Polish language.

Some Polish words may sound familiar. See if you can guess what these Polish words mean in English.

lampa   matematyka   mleko   muzyka
(See page 32 for answers.)

Learning Polish

The Polish alphabet is similar to the English alphabet. However, there are no letters q, v, or x. The Polish language also uses special marks called diacritics to make some extra letters.

a ą b c ć d
e ę f g h i j
k l ł m n ń
o ó p r s ś
t u w y z ź ż

diacritic

Some letters in Polish are sounded, or pronounced, differently from English. Below are some examples.

c	sounds like "ts"	*co* (what) is pronounced "tsoh"
w	sounds like "v"	*wyspa* (island) is pronounced "vis-pah"
j	sounds like "y"	*jeden* (one) is pronounced "yed-en"
cż	sounds like "ch"	*czas* (time) is pronounced "chahs"

Saying Hello and Goodbye

In Poland people greet each other in many ways. Some shake hands. Some kiss each others' cheeks or give a hug. Others nod and smile.

How to say it
kiss = *pocałunek*
hug = *uścisk*
smile = *uśmiech*

Polish speakers might say "*cześć*"
("hi"). At the end of the day people
might say "*do widzenia*" ("goodbye")
or "*dobranoc*" ("goodnight").

Talking About Yourself

If you are speaking Polish, the first thing you might do is introduce yourself: *"Mam na imię …"* ("My name is …"). Then you might say to someone *"Bardzo mi miło"* ("Pleased to meet you").

How to say it
My name is … = *Mam na imię …*
Pleased to meet you = *Bardzo mi miło*

"*Mówię po polsku*" means "I speak Polish." But if someone speaks too quickly, you might reply "*Nie rozumiem*" ("I do not understand").

Asking About Others

When meeting someone for the first time you might ask, *"Jak masz na imię?"* ("What is your name?") You might also ask *"Skąd jesteś?"* ("Where are you from?")

What is your name? = *Jak masz na imię?*
Where are you from? = *Skąd jesteś?*

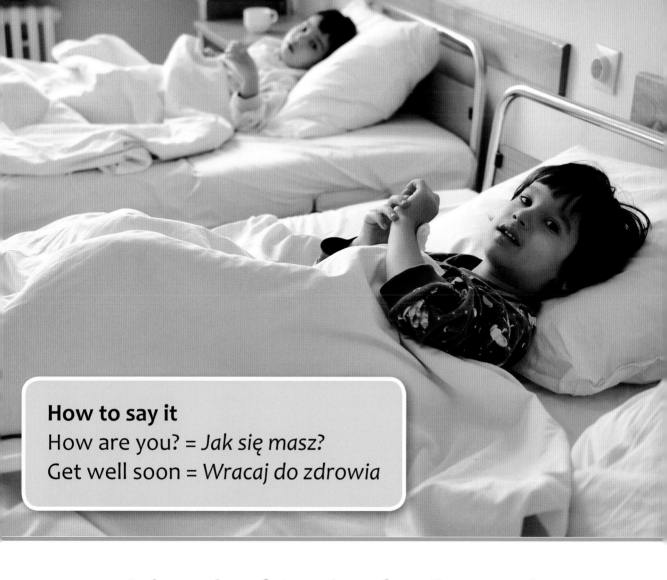

You might ask a friend or family member
"*Jak się masz?*" ("How are you?")
If someone is sick you could say
"*Wracaj do zdrowia.*" ("Get well soon.")

At Home

In Poland people may live in apartments or in large houses. They might live in big, busy cities such as Kraków or Warsaw.

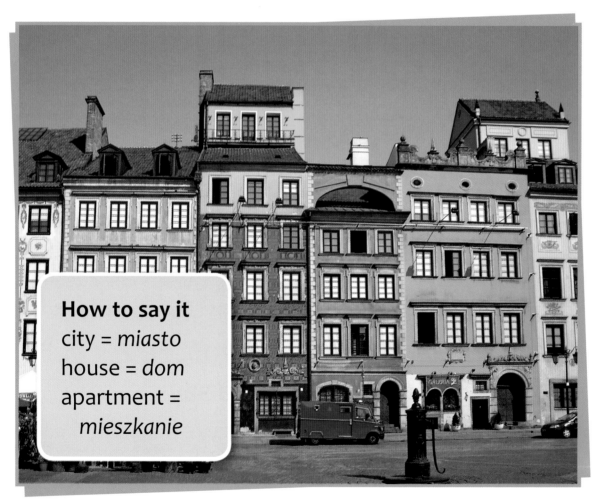

How to say it
city = *miasto*
house = *dom*
apartment = *mieszkanie*

How to say it
village = *wioska*
farm = *gospodarstwo*
horse = *koń*
chicken = *kurczę*

Poland also has many villages. People farm the land and grow apples, pears, and plums. They also raise horses, geese, and chickens.

Family Life

Families in Poland are like families in many other countries. Often parents and children have other relatives living with them. These might include grandparents or aunts and uncles.

How to say it
father = *ojciec*
mother = *matka*
children = *dzieci*

How to say it
brother = *brat*
sister = *siostra*
game = *gra*
fun = *zabawa*

People in Poland enjoy watching television, and using computers and cell phones. Children enjoy playing outdoor games, such as *klasy* and *chłopek*. These games are like hopscotch.

At School

Children in Poland have to go to school from the age of 6 to 18. Some of their classes are in math, science, and history. They also learn other languages, such as English, German, and Russian.

How to say it
school = *szkoła*
pupil = *uczeń*
school bag = *teczka szkolna*

How to say it
teacher = *nauczyciel*
languages = *języki*
history = *historia*

Polish children learn about famous Polish writers and artists. These include the writer Joseph Conrad and the musician Frederic Chopin.

Sports and Dancing

People in Poland enjoy soccer. The national team plays at the Silesian Stadium. Polish people also like to play ice hockey, go cycling, and watch motorcycle racing.

How to say it
soccer = *piłka nożna*
ice hockey = *hokej na lodzie*

How to say it
dancer (male) = *tancerz*
dancer (female) = *tancerka*

Dances from long ago are popular in Poland. People all over the world like to learn these dances. They include the *mazurek*, a lively dance, and the *polonez*, a slower dance.

Polish food usually contains lots of meat, vegetables, and cream. A popular Polish food is the *pierogi*. This is a baked dumpling stuffed with potato and cheese, and other food, such as mushrooms.

How to say it
potato = *kartofel*
cheese = *ser*
mushrooms = *grzyby*

cheesecake

How to say it
cake = *ciasto*
meat = *mięso*
cabbage = *kapusta*

Another Polish favorite food is *bigos*, a stew made of meat and cabbage. Polish desserts include cheesecake and apple tarts.

Clothes and Shopping

Years ago women in Poland wore flowered dresses and bead necklaces. Men wore embroidered jackets. Today, Polish people wear modern clothes such as jeans.

How to say it
dress = *suknia*
jacket = *marynarka*
jeans = *dżinsy*
necklace = *naszyjnik*

How to say it
market = *rynek*
shopping center = *centrum handlowe*

Some people in Poland shop in village markets, while others shop in large shopping centers. Polish craftspeople make and sell beautiful jewelry.

29

Pronunciation Guide

English	Polish	Pronunciation
apartment	mieszkanie	MHEE-SHKAH-NHEEH
brother	brat	BRAHT
cabbage	kapusta	KAH-PUH-STAH
cake	ciasto	CHEE-AH-STOH
cheese	ser	SEHR
chicken	kurczę	koor-CHAN
children	dzieci	DZHEE-chee
city	miasto	MEEAH-STOH
dancer (female)	tancerka	TAN-THEHR-KAH
dancer (male)	tancerz	TAN-tsesh
dress	suknia	SOOK-neeah
farm	gospodarstwo	gos-poh-DAR-stvoh
father	ojciec	oy-CHETS
fun	zabawa	zah-BAH-vah
game	gra	grah
Get well soon	Wracaj do zdrowia	VRA-tsay doh ZDROH-veeah
goodbye	do widzenia	DOH vee-DZEH-nah
goodnight	dobranoc	do-BRAH-nots
hi	cześć	CHESHCH
history	historia	hee-STOH-reeah
horse	koń	KOHN
house	dom	DOHM
How are you?	Jak się masz?	YAK seh MUSH
hug	uścisk	OOSEE-tsehsk
I do not understand	Nie rozumiem	NHEE roh-ZOO-meehm
I speak Polish	Mówię po polsku	MOO-vieh poh POHL-skooh
ice hockey	hokej na lodzie	HOH-key nah loh-dzhee
jacket	marynarka	mah-rih-NAHR-kah
jeans	dżinsy	DZHEEN-SIH

30

kiss	pocałunek	poh-tsah-WOO-nehk
lamp	lampa	LAM-pah
languages	języki	yehn-sih-kih
market	rynek	RIH-nehk
mathematics	matematyka	mah-teh-MAH-ti-kah
meat	mięso	MEEHN-soh
milk	mleko	MLEH-koh
mother	matka	MAHT-kah
mushrooms	grzyby	GZHIH-bih
music	muzyka	mooh-SIH-kah
My name is . . .	Mam na imię . . .	MAHM nah EE-meeh
necklace	naszyjnik	nah-SHIY-kneek
Pleased to meet you	Bardzo mi miło	BAHR-dzhoh mee MEE-woh
potato	kartofel	kahr-TOH-fell
pupil	uczeń	OO-chehn
school	szkoła	SHKOH-wah
school bag	teczka szkolna	TEHCH-kah SHKOHL-nah
shopping center	centrum handlowe	TSEN-troom hahn-DLOH-veh
sister	siostra	SIOH-strah
smile	uśmiech	OOSEEH-meeh
soccer	piłka nożna	PEEW-kah NOSH-nah
teacher	nauczyciel	nah-oo-CHIH-tzeel
village	wioska	VYOH-skah
What is your name?	Jak masz na imię?	YAHK MASH nah EE-meeh
Where are you from?	Skąd jesteś?	ZKOHNT YEHS-tesh

Find Out More

Book

Parker, Vic. *A Visit to Poland*. Chicago: Heinemann Library, 2008.

Website

kids.nationalgeographic.com/kids/places/find/poland/

Index

Meanings of the words on page 9

lampa = lamp

mleko = milk

matematyka = mathematics

muzyka = music